No Compromise, No Political Trading
Wilhelm Liebknecht

Contents

Part 1

PREFACE

The following pamphlet is not an address, as was my first one on Tactics [1]; but it is occasioned by an address which I delivered this summer, at the request of my Berlin constituents, on the last Bavarian legislative elections in particular and on compromises in general. For some time past and from different directions persistent efforts have been made to bring our party nearer to the other political parties; this, together with the incessant demand for taking part in the Prussian legislative elections, has aroused in a part of the Berlin voters, as well as among the comrades all over Germany, an apprehension that there may exist in the party certain tendencies which, though not having that aim, nevertheless must have the result, of leading the Social Democratic party over into the field of spoils politics, pure and simple. This apprehension was nourished by Bernstein's book of repentance, a solemn renunciation of social democratic principles by a comrade who up to that time had been considered a guardian of our principles, and by his recantation of the social democratic heresy and his reconfession of faith in the bourgeois philosophy as the only means of salvation. Bernstein's pamphlet in itself is insignificant and contains not a single new, original idea, but merely acknowledges as correct what the enemies of the Social Democracy for decades past have said against it a hundred times; yet, taken in connection with the confusing agitation for taking part in the Prussian legislative elections and with the unfortunate Isegrim articles against the militia system and in favor of militarism, the pamphlet, considered as a symptom, acquired an importance which could not be ignored.

The party was engaged in a fight against the penitentiary bill, and other attempts at coercion on the part of the dominant reactionists, and was just beginning to forget Schippelism and Bernsteinism, expecting from the next party convention a thorough shaking up and cleaning out, when suddenly the report came of the political "cow-trade" or log-rolling in Bavaria. We have been accustomed to Bavarian peculiarities for years; we know that Bavarian affairs, and in general South German affairs, are not to be measured according to the North German standard; and no one can be more tolerant than the Berlin comrades who, in front of the gates of the Imperial Capital, have to deal with peculiarities which, though of a different kind, are quite as striking as the Bavarian possibly can be. We know particularly that where the religious element cuts a figure in politics and the clerical Center party prevents a normal political development, class-consciousness is easily crowded out by other considerations. And also outside of Bavaria we have heard of some very strange campaign alliances. Nevertheless, what happened this time in Bavaria was in its way an innovation. A formal alliance was entered into, not underhanded, not over the heads of the mass by particular comrades, but by one party with another party, by the leaders of the Social Democracy in Bavaria, with the leaders of the Center party in Bavaria.

This event stirred up a great commotion and caused the most intense anxiety everywhere in party circles. At first the astonishment, the disapproval, found no expression. As the legislative elections in Bavaria are indirect, one could not immediately raise a protest, for in so doing one would only have embarrassed the Bavarian comrades, who were then in the midst of the fight, and would perhaps have incurred a grave responsibility. Therefore, the Bavarian supporters of the political cow trade had the field to themselves for the time being. Under such circumstances, it is easy to understand that the apprehensions of comrades, who thought they saw indications of a designed and methodical stagnation of the party, were aroused to the utmost. Berlin comrades turned to me. I explained why the **Vorwaerts** had not yet taken a stand towards the Bavarian cow trade, but made no secret of the fact that my views on compromises were not the same as those of the editorial staff; I wrote an article, which in spite of its unusually calm tone, was looked upon by the Bavarian comrades as a grievous attack; I also explained my views in a meeting of the voters' club of the Sixth Berlin election district. Although, for the sake of sweet peace, I prevented a vote of censure for the Bavarian comrades, nevertheless both myself and the Berlin comrades were, on account of this meeting, violently attacked by the Bavarian party members, and not always in elegant terms. One who feels that he is in the wrong generally makes up for the weakness of his case by the violence of his speech. I have always taken the insolence of my opponents as an involuntary compliment, and never bothered myself about it.

About the time of the Bavarian cow trade the entrance of a socialist – Millerand – into a reactionary bourgeois cabinet took place in France and was the cause of a split in the French Social Democracy. The ablest of our French comrades, – Guesde, Lafargue and Vaillant, the founders of the modern socialist movement in France, – protested against the entrance of Millerand into the cabinet of the reactionary capitalist, Waldeck-Rousseau, and of Gallifet, the butcher of the Communists; they withdrew from the socialist group, which they were convinced had abandoned the platform of the class

4

struggle.

Here we could see the dangers of a compromise policy in their life-size and entire outlines. In the meantime an article appeared in **Vorwaerts**, in the issue of July 28, entitled *Momentary Alliances*, which sought to justify the compromise policy. I therefore determined, at the request of comrades in Berlin and vicinity, to write a pamphlet and express myself, as I know, in harmony with an overwhelming majority of the Berlin comrades, on the question of tactics, especially on compromises and alliances; and thus, so far as in my power lies, afford the party an opportunity, before the party convention is held, to realize in their proper connection and in their entire extent the consequences which an abandonment of the time-tried policy of our party would bring about.

When I speak here of our policy, I use the word without regard to anything immaterial and superficial, but in the sense which since the beginning of the party it has had for us in contrast to all other parties, – in the sense of the policy of the class struggle, which has very often changed in form, but in substance has remained the same, – our unique proletarian class policy, which separates us from all other political parties in the world of bourgeois society and excludes us from intercourse with them.

The pamphlet is a vacation task. It was written on the move in the true sense of the word, in house and field, on mountains, in the cars, here and there. This, of course, necessarily marred its unity, but shows also how seriously I took the matter, to sacrifice for it the quiet of my vacation.

THE PARTY LAW

The question of compromises has, in one form or another, engaged the attention of our party ever since its entrance into the political arena. But I have not now the time nor is this the place for a complete historical presentation of the subject. The present state of party law in reference to the compromise question is expressed in the resolutions of the party conventions held at Cologne, Hamburg and Stuttgart. The resolution of the Cologne convention, passed October 28, 1893, is as follows:

"Whereas, The three-class electoral system of Prussia, which, according to Bismarck's own expression, is the most wretched of all systems of election, makes it impossible for the Social Democracy to take an independent part in the elections for the Prussian legislature with any prospect of success; and whereas, it contradicts the principles heretofore followed by the party in elections to enter into compromises with hostile parties, because this would necessarily lead to demoralization and to strife and dissension in the ranks of the party; therefore, resolved, that it is the duty of the party members in Prussia to abstain from participation in the election for the legislature.

And whereas, the electoral systems in the separate states constitute an excellent specimen of reactionary election laws and particularly the plutocratic character of the three-class electoral system in Prussia makes it impossible for the laboring class to send its own representatives to the legislature; therefore, the convention calls upon the party members to begin a systematic and energetic agitation in all the separate states for the introduction of universal, equal, secret and direct suffrage in elections for the legislature as demanded by our party platform."

6

Four years later, on October 9, 1897, the Hamburg convention passed the following resolution:

"The resolution of the Cologne convention forbidding the Prussian members of the party to participate in the legislative elections under the three-class system of voting, is repealed. Participation in the next Prussian legislative elections is recommended everywhere where the conditions render it possible for the party members to do so. Just how far it is possible to take part in the elections in the separate election districts must be decided by the party members of each election district according to local circumstances.

Compromises and alliances with other parties must not be entered into."

The repeal of the Cologne resolution was passed by 160 votes against 50. The entire resolution was passed by 145 votes against 64, one delegate not voting.

After the vote on the separate parts of the resolution and after the vote on the whole, in order to prevent any question from arising as to the practical meaning of the Hamburg resolution, the chairman, Singer, with the express consent of Bebel, who had offered the resolution, and without objection by anyone, and with unanimous consent, entered on the minutes, made the following announcement:

"I wish to state that the convention is unanimous in the view that under the resolution adopted here no participation in the elections can take place except by putting up social democratic candidates."

That comrades should, in the first instance, vote for candidates of the liberal party was, as Bebel remarked, absolutely excluded, and would belong under the head of compromises and alliances with other parties.

In spite of the clear language of the resolution and of the clear and authoritative interpretation thereof on a point susceptible of different constructions, the convention had hardly adjourned when differences of opinion began to be expressed. In sharp contradiction to the facts and to the record of the proceedings, it was denied that voting in the first instance by our party for candidates of the liberal party would be a compromise; and the claim was even made that the convention had been bulldozed by Singer.

Last year's convention was held at Stuttgart immediately before the elections for the Prussian legislature. There was such a difference of opinion that it was not possible to think of disposing of the matter, especially as the order of business before the convention was overloaded without that. So nothing could be done but leave the final disposition of the matter for a future convention, and for the present pass an emergency resolution.

On October 5, 1898, the Stuttgart convention adopted unanimously the following resolution, agreed upon by a committee, to wit:

"Participation in the Prussian legislative elections under the three-class electoral system cannot be regarded, as is the case in elections for the Reichstag, as a marshaling of forces; it is not a means of attaining a moral effect by the number of our votes, but is only a means of attaining certain practical results, especially warding off the danger of allowing the most hide-bound reactionists to get a majority in the legislature. Proceeding from this view, the convention declares that participation in the Prussian legislative elections is not required in all election districts, the less so as the shortness of the time which remains before the Prussian legislative elections makes it impossible to bring together the widely divergent views now existing within the party on this question, so to make harmonious action by the party possible. Under these circumstances the convention leaves it to the comrades of the separate election districts to decide on the question of participation. If it is decided in an election district to take part, and if a proposition is made to support candidates of our political opponents, then the candidates must pledge themselves, in case of their election to the legislature, to work for the introduction of the universal, equal, direct and secret ballot, for the elections to the legislature, the same as it now exists for the elections to the Reichstag, and to resist energetically all measures in the legislature which tend to diminish or abolish the existing rights of the people in the separate states. All propositions introduced under the head of 'Prussian Legislative Elections' shall be considered disposed of by the adoption of this resolution."

This was the Stuttgart resolution. As can be seen, it is only temporary and leaves the question of tactics exactly on the basis of the Hamburg resolution. In spite of that, the comrades of some election districts considered themselves justified in making, contrary to this resolution, arrangements with other parties which were clearly compromises within the meaning of the Hamburg resolution. And the latest events in Bavaria, the alliance with the Center party, which was characterised as a cow trade by the comrades themselves, who took part in it, has shown that when once the thin end of the opportunist wedge has forced itself into the policy of the party the thick end soon follows.

PROLETARIAN SOCIALISM

For our party and for our party tactics there is but one valid basis: the basis of the class struggle, out of which the Social Democratic party has sprung up, and out of which alone it can draw the necessary strength to bid defiance to every storm and to all its enemies. The founders of our party, – Marx, Engels and Lassalle, – impressed upon the workingmen the necessity of the class character of our movement so deeply that down to a very recent time there were no considerable deviations or getting off the track. The Cologne resolution was called forth by a proposal made by Edward Bernstein, then living in London, and as editor of the **Social Democrat** honored by the members of the party.

Till the year 1893 there never was any talk in public about the possibility or advisability of taking part in the Prussian legislative elections. In the beginning of the '80s, the co-operation of the Social Democracy with the political democrats was advocated on the quiet by the democrats of Frankfort for the purpose of gaining a socialist and a democratic representative for Frankfort in the legislature; but the proposition was declined, also on the quiet, without getting noised abroad. What turned the scale was this consideration, viz.: *That the class character of the party would be weakened by an alliance of this kind*; and that the advantage of gaining a representative would be far more than offset by the disadvantage of an alliance in a legislative election with a party which we are compelled to fight in the Reichstag election. The importance of a seat in the Prussian legislature was not overlooked by anyone. But it was looked upon as more important that the representatives of the party should depend exclusively upon the strength of the party, and not upon an alliance with parties which might have momentarily a common interest with us, but which in their political make-up are hostile to us and will remain permanently hostile.

Bernstein's proposal, which contemplated a participation of the Social Democracy in the Prussian legislative elections, found little response and no advocates; so that the resolution introduced and supported by Bebel against such participation was adopted unanimously.

That the question of taking part in the Prussian legislative elections should come up again after many years and even lead to quite animated debates, appears at first sight unintelligible. But it is explained by two circumstances which I will here set forth.

First. In reference to the Prussian three-class electoral system the views of many of the comrades had in the course of time undergone a change. It had escaped the memory of some of them, here and there, that the logically and cunningly realized purpose of the three-class electoral system was to exclude with hermetic sealing all democratic thought and sentiment, and that the capitalistic era, which began about the same time with the introduction of the "most wretched of all electoral systems," had by creating a class conscious proletariat rendered the vote of the socialist masses more insignificant than the vote of the democratic masses had been originally. How badly many of the speakers (both men and women) at the Hamburg convention deceived themselves as to the working of the three-class electoral system is clear from the fact that some of them entertained the delusion that the reform of the Prussian legislative elections could be used as the means of a grand arousing of the masses. In the jubilation over the success which had been achieved under other non-democratic laws regulating legislative elections, especially in Saxony, many had forgotten that the Prussian three-class system made the publicity of the ballot obligatory, and thereby in advance practically disfranchised all who were dependent, either economically, socially or politically, that is, the great majority of the population, and by this means alone rendered it impossible for the masses to take part in the election or get up any general enthusiasm.

The optimistic self-deception in regard to the three-class electoral law went so far that not a few of the comrades imagined in all seriousness that we social democrats would be in a position by our own strength without fusion or even an alliance with other parties, to win a number, if only a small number, of seats. To-day no one is laboring under this delusion any longer. To-day everybody knows that we cannot win a single seat in the Prussian legislature without a compromise or an alliance. It was different two years ago when the party convention, its majority being under the curse of optimistic self-deception, pronounced in favor of taking part in the Prussian legislative elections. Fortunately, however, the heads and supreme council of the party bethought themselves of the origin and nature of the party and by an unqualified prohibition of all compromises and alliances with other parties sought to prevent the self-deception from causing steps which might injure the party and lead it astray into wrong paths.

The Hamburg resolution has been called contradictory and illogical. True, if the party the same as before rejected all compromises and alliances with other parties, then there was no sense in repealing the Cologne resolution. The contradiction is explained, as already indicated, by the fact that a portion of the party deceived itself or was deceived as to the nature of the Prussian three-class election law. But from this contradiction to conclude, as has actually been done, that the party had more at

12

heart its desire to participate in the Prussian legislative elections than its aversion to compromises, and that therefore, as a contradiction existed, it must be solved by unqualifiedly advocating participation in the elections and by repealing the prohibition against compromises and election alliances; such a conclusion gives evidence of just as little logic as of regard for the principles and history of the party.

Second. This brings me to the second reason why the question of participation in the legislative elections could become a matter of serious party strife. In certain circles there exists an inclination, or let us say an effort, to desert the platform of the class struggle and enter into the common arena of the other parties. As all the other parties stand upon the basis of a political state, therefore their field of activity is necessarily confined to the spoils of politics. I do not say that the advocates of the new tactics all wish this: as to some of them I am convinced that they do not wish it. But others wish it; and it is no mere accident that it was just Bernstein who first proposed the participation of the social democracy in the Prussian legislative elections. This tactics corresponds perfectly with Bernstein's program which aims at the politicalization of the Social Democracy; whereas, it is decidedly illogical from the standpoint of those who do not wish to deny or destroy the militant character of our party as carrying on a class struggle.

STATE CAPITALISM

I do not hesitate to repeat my former declaration that a practical surrender of our party principles appears to me far more dangerous than all of Bernstein's theoretical will-o'-the-wisps put together. It has been claimed that in the spoils parties political nerve has died out; that they have lost the spirit of freedom and justice. The claim certainly does not lack foundation, and yet that condition is no recent matter. Disregarding short periods, the German bourgeoisie never did have what is understood by "political nerve." But however that may be, it cannot be denied that we are now living under the influence of politico-economic conditions which tend to sharpen in the highest degree the economic and political antagonisms on the one hand, and yet on the other hand tend towards an opportunist relaxation of principles. In addition to that we must take into consideration the political backwardness of the bourgeoisie in Germany, which is the cause of the fact that there does not exist here a really liberal party, to say nothing of a democratic party. This fact has this as its natural result: that the honestly liberal and democratic elements of the bourgeoisie gravitate more and more towards the side of the Social Democracy as the only party which is fighting for democratic principles in Germany. But these democratic elements do not thereby become Socialists, though many believe they are socialists. In short, we have now in Germany a phenomenon which has been observable in France for half a century and longer, and which has contributed much to the confusion of party relations in France, viz.: that a part of the radical bourgeoisie rallies around the Socialist flag without understanding the nature of socialism. This political socialism, which in fact is only philanthropic humanitarian radicalism, has retarded the development of socialism in France exceedingly. It has diluted and blurred the principles and weakened the socialist party because it brought into it troops upon which no reliance could be placed in the decisive moment.

Marx in his articles on the class struggles in France [2]

characterized for us this political socialism. And it would be an unparalleled case of flying the track and going astray if the German Social Democracy, which has had such wonderful success and such a wonderful growth for the very reason that it has marched ahead unterrified on the basis of the class struggle, should suddenly face about and plunge into mistakes, the avoidance of which has been the power and pride of our party, and has put the German Social Democracy at the head of the international social democracy of all countries.

The disappearance of fear and aversion to us in political circles of course brings political elements into our ranks. As long as this takes place on a small scale it causes no apprehension because the political elements are outnumbered by the proletarian elements and are gradually assimilated. But it is a different thing if the political elements in the party become so numerous and influential that their assimilation becomes difficult and even the danger arises that the proletarian socialist element will be crowded to the rear. This danger of politicalization threatens the German Social Democracy from two sources on account of the backwardness of our bourgeoisie. First, the democratic elements of the bourgeoisie, which find no political satisfaction in their own class, flow to us in greater numbers than in countries with a normally developed bourgeoisie; second, the bureaucratic, though capitalistic, spirit of our governments tends towards a state socialism which, in fact, is only state capitalism, but which is dazzling and misleading for those who are easily deceived by external similarities and catch words. The German, or more accurately the Prussian, state socialism whose ideal is a military, landlord and police state, hates democracy above everything else. The Kanitzes and their followers claim to be out and out radical socialists, but will have nothing to do with democracy. Democracy is their enemy. It is to them something inherently political. But all politics is diametrically opposed to what is socialist. So by this trick logic we arrive at the conclusion which has gained footing here and there, even in social democratic circles, that democracy as savoring of politics has nothing in common with socialism, but on the contrary is opposed to it. Certain errors, for example the opposition to the militia system, can be traced to this piece of sophistry, as also at one time the false teachings of von Schweitzer. But the truth is that democracy is not a thing that is specifically political, and we must never forget that we are not merely a socialist party, but a social democratic party because we have perceived that socialism and democracy are inseparable.

BISMARCK

As Prince Bismarck, in the '60s, wanted to move the "Acheron" of socialism, and through the intervention of Brass offered to me the editorship of the **North German Gazette**, and then later through Bucher offered to Marx even the editorship of the **Staats Anzeiger**, in both cases with full freedom to advocate socialism unreservedly, clear down to its ultimate consequences, it was of course not love for socialism or knowledge of socialism that led Prince Bismarck to do this. He understood nothing about socialism at that time, and never did understand anything about it down to his death; in fact, he never had any conception of the moving forces of political and social life at all. There probably never lived at any time in any country a "statesman" who was less scientific, who had less knowledge, and who relied so purely on experience and a sort of half-gambler, half-peddler cunning, as Bismarck. Those

16

offers to socialists place in the clearest light the untruthfulness of Prince Bismarck's claim that he always regarded the social democracy as incompatible with the existence of the state. Bismarck wanted to use socialism for the purpose of breaking up and dissolving the bourgeois liberal opposition, especially the Progressive party. This, in itself, is the most conclusive proof that he had no conception of the real nature of socialism. Of course the fate of the boy magician was repeated. The elemental force which was conjured up grew over the head of the dabbler, and he did not get the best of socialism; socialism got the best of him.

The question of tactics came up then in our party for the first time. Should we, in consideration of certain concessions to the laborers, aid Bismarck against the Progressive party and other opponents of his policy in the expectation of being then after that strong enough for a successful struggle against him and against the landlord, police and military state embodied in his person? Or did prudence and party interest demand that we, taking advantage of Bismarck's quarrel with the Progressive bourgeoisie and the other opponents of his policy, contest the Bismarckian policy and organize the proletariat into an independent political party for the purpose of preparing it for the conquest of political power?

For a while the proletariat wavered, but after a few years the tactics, advocated principally by Herr von Schweitzer, of drawing closer to the Bismarckian policy, was given up and the tactics was everywhere accepted which has ever since been in force for the party down to the present day. *This tactics consists in keeping clear the class character of the socialist party as a proletarian party; to train it by agitation, education and organization for the victorious completion of the emancipation struggle; to wage a systematic war against the class state*, in whose hands the political and economic power of capitalism is concentrated, and in this war to draw advantages as far as possible out of the quarrels and conflicts of the different political parties with each other.

BOURGEOIS AND BOURGEOISIE

In Germany the bourgeoisie has never attained political power as in France and England. Though the English bourgeoisie two and a half centuries ago, and the French bourgeoisie more than a century ago, cleared away all the medieval rubbish, the German bourgeoisie has never yet been in the position to bring about a political revolution and to realize in the state what is called political liberty. The loss of the world's commerce in consequence of the discovery of America, and in connection with that the stunting of industrial activity; the political splitting up and ruin of Germany; the paralysis of the national spirit bordering almost on death; the rise of dynastic interests hostile to the people and to enlightenment; all these prevented the growth of a strong citizenry. As in 1848 a belated opportunity was offered, the German people even then did not have the strength for a political revolution. After a brief revel of freedom it bowed its head again under the old yoke. From fear of the laborers, in whom it scented a new and dangerous power, it became reactionary, without ever having been revolutionary; it did penance for its dreams of freedom, which appeared to it as youthful indiscretions, and threw itself into the arms of political reactionism, filled with but one remaining ideal, viz.: to get rich. The citizen disappeared from the political arena and became either politically indifferent or else capitalistic. And to be capitalistic means to recognize and support the government unconditionally, provided it is a class government and represents and promotes exclusively the interests of capitalism.

To prevent misunderstandings and wrong impressions, we must become fully conscious of the difference between "political" and "capitalistic." These two ideas, which because of the ambiguity of the German word "*Buerger*" are very easily confused by us, must be clearly separated from each other. In France the word "*bourgeois*," which in the middle ages had the same meaning as our "*Buerger*," in the course of time and of economic development gradually assumed the meaning of "great-capitalist;" whereas we Germans for this latter idea borrow the French word "*bourgeois*," but also use concurrently the German words "*Buerger*," and "*buergerlich*" without noticing the difference. So there arises a confusion of language which is anything but conducive to clearness of conception. We speak of "*buergerlich*" society, and mean modern capitalistic bourgeois society. We speak of "*buergerlich*" spirit, "*buergerlich*" freedom, and mean a democratic spirit of freedom such as the citizenry had in former times when it was fighting the priests and feudal landlords, which spirit, however, is diametrically opposed to the spirit of the capitalistic, and hence reactionary, landlord and priest coddling citizenry, or bourgeoisie of to-day.

The correctness of the so-called materialistic conception of history, which considers the political development as dependent on the economic, cannot be brought more strikingly and convincingly to the mind than by the change which in the course of the Nineteenth century has been wrought in the bourgeoisie. It can be demonstrated with the greatest precision how with the change in the productive relations a change of political view and attitude has taken place in the bourgeoisie. Every step forward in economic development has been a step forward in the development of class antagonisms and a step in the approach of the bourgeoisie towards its old enemies, the landlords and priests, and a step in drawing away from the rising proletariat, which in order to effect its emancipation, must advocate equal rights for all men and the democratic principles formerly supported by the bourgeoisie. *The moment the proletariat steps forth as a class separate from the bourgeoisie and having interests opposed to it, from that moment the bourgeoisie ceased to be democratic.* In the states of the European continent this reaction falls in a characteristic manner just in a period which is usually called the revolutionary period par excellence – in the period of the February and March revolutions. The contradiction is only an apparent one. The February revolution was a tardy victory of bourgeois idealism which stirred up the material interests of bourgeois realism to contradiction, to opposition and to reaction. The premature outbreak of the proletarian revolution (in the battle of June, 1848, at Paris), which followed upon the heels of the belated outbreak of the bourgeois revolution, drove the bourgeoisie over to the side of its hereditary enemy, because it foresaw in the victory of the proletariat the downfall of capitalism. In France Napoleon was elected President, and in Germany the bourgeoisie even in the honeymoon of the March revolution longed for a deliverer which would down the red specter. Thus the "black reaction," which in 1849 followed our revolution, was in fact simply the true character of this revolution, stripped of its fantastic deceptive dress of gilded phrases. *Under the rule of capitalism the bourgeoisie was forced to become politically reactionary* so far as it was capitalistic or stood under capitalistic influence. The "black reaction" which half a century ago spread over the European continent, was just as much a historical necessity as the still

20

blacker reaction of the present zigzag policy of penitentiary bills which capitalism in a fit of desperation has forced upon us.

THE GERMAN BOURGEOISIE NEVER PASSED THROUGH
THE LIBERAL STAGE OF DEVELOPMENT

In Germany where capitalism was developed later than in England and France, and where it was not preceded, as in those two countries, by an era of economic prosperity for the bourgeoisie as well as of political supremacy by it, the whole political development was obliged to take on a different character. There a soil cleared of medieval mould and undergrowth; here, the most modern of modern conditions, as modern as in France and England, in between medieval mould and undergrowth; the healthy growth entwined with ivy which sucks the life out of everything that it clasps with its tendrils; which only lives from death and rottenness and which most be torn off and grubbed up to prevent the healthy and growing from being sacrificed to the dead. The German bourgeoisie, which was sleeping the sleep of impotence at the time when in other lands the bourgeoisie impressed upon the state its bourgeois character, does not even now possess the strength to tear away and extirpate the romantic and death-bringing parasitic ivy of landlordism and medieval semi-barbarism.

The political impotence of the German citizenry in past and present is what distinguishes the political life of Germany from that of the other advanced countries, and has assigned to the German proletariat the mission not only of solving its own strictly proletarian problem, but also of accomplishing the work left undone by our bourgeoisie. Tactics is determined by the nature of the conditions. So far as the bourgeoisie is capitalistic, we have to fight it; so far as the bourgeoisie opposes capitalism and the reactionism which it shields and assists, we have either to support it positively or at least not assume a hostile attitude towards it, unless it gets in our line of fire, as for example, in the elections for the Reichstag where a bourgeois and a social democratic candidate are running against each other.

Disregarding the von Schweitzer episode, the German Social Democracy has consistently and consciously followed the tactics prescribed in the **Communist Manifesto**, to direct its main attack against political reactionism and to lend aid to the bourgeoisie, so far as it is liberal or democratic, in its struggle against political reactionism and in no case to throw itself on the side of political reaction in its struggle against the bourgeoisie. It is necessary to emphasize this, because Bernstein in his polemic written against the Social Democratic Party of Germany, and which has been so suspiciously praised and recommended, has accused us of something which is a favorite old legend of Eugene Richter's, viz.: that we blindly opposed the German bourgeoisie to the advantage of political reactionism and repelled and terrorized it so much that in its alarm it took refuge under the wings of a reactionary landlord, police and military state. It is not possible to slap the truth squarer in the face than is done by saying this.

THE FAILURE OF THE PROGRESSIVE PARTY

At the time of the great constitutional struggle in the '60s there was no socialist party worth speaking of. In 1864, at the time

Lassalle was killed in a duel with the Wallachian noble Rakowitz, the Universal German Working Men's Union numbered in all Germany 5,000 or 6,000 members on paper; in reality still fewer. This little band could not have scared the German Progressive party out of its wits, even though we measure the latter's valor by the microscopic scale of rabbit courage, befitting the German bourgeoisie. Yet it surrendered to Bismarck; and after the success of the civil war of 1866 it granted him indemnity and bowed itself under the Caudine yoke which he set up. To claim that the Social Democracy is to blame for that is simply ridiculous. It is true that Lassalle had attacked the bourgeoisie very bitterly, but in so doing had found very little sympathy among German workingmen. And although Lassalle in his opposition to the Progressive party occasionally got perhaps somewhat too close to the Bismarckian reactionary policy, still it must not be forgotten that at the beginning of the constitutional struggle he had stood on the side of the Progressive party and only separated from it after it had obstinately refused to carry on the struggle in earnest in spite of his repeated demands that it do so.

The German bourgeoisie – and this is the key to its otherwise unaccountable conduct – did not have in 1862 any more than it had in 1848 and earlier, the stuff for a political revolution. It feared – as I told one of the leaders of the Progressive party to his face in the beginning of the year 1863 – *it feared a revolution more than a reaction*. And Bismarck with his cynical contempt of men and his horse-trader cuteness, soon brought out that fact. The Progressists did not strike him as "imposing;" and the more impudent he was in his intercourse with them the easier he curled them around his finger. To hold the German Social Democracy responsible for the treason to liberty committed by the Prussian Progressive party is not only an insult to historical truth; it indicates also a complete misunderstanding of the role which the German bourgeoisie has played since the middle ages.

I simply put the two facts side by side: In the period of the constitutional struggle when the Progressive party stood at the height of its power and had the people behind it, Bismarck, then in the beginning of his career, turned it down with the greatest ease. In the period of the anti-Socialist law, when Bismarck stood at the height of his power and with all the resources of capitalism was exercising a bourgeois dictatorship, he was turned down by the Social Democracy with the greatest ease, though it had all the political parties against it. That shows who can fight reactionism in Germany and who can not.

The wretchedness of the German bourgeoisie does not, however, release us front the duty of assisting it, wherever it does earnestly oppose reactionism, provided our own interests do not thereby suffer. And this has been done without exception ever since the German Social Democracy entered the arena as an independent party. For myself, I need only to mention the fact that in 1865 I was expelled from Prussia because I foiled Bismarck's attempt to crush the Progressive party with the aid of the Socialists as between two millstones. I can say with a good conscience that in all my struggles against the Bismarckian reaction I have fought for political liberty. And in my oft-quoted pamphlet on the political attitude of the Social Democracy I emphasized the democratic character of our movement not less than has been done recently by Bernstein, who recommends to us as brand new wisdom what we have already been practicing for thirty-odd years.

THE PAMPHLET ON TACTICS

I must here say a word about my above mentioned pamphlet on tactics. The speech out of which it arose was delivered in the year 1869 at the time of the North German Confederation; this was a temporary arrangement which could not possibly last and which would have to end either with the breaking down of Bismarck's Great-Prussian policy or with its victory by a union with the South German States, excepting Austria. In this temporary state or interim the tactics forced upon us by the logic of the facts was that of opposition at any price. Bismarck had introduced a universal suffrage of the Napoleonic pattern, not to establish the sovereignty of the people, but to cover up his despotic dictatorship. As Napoleon through his prefects directed the universal suffrage as he pleased, so Bismarck thought he could do the same through his local counsellors. It seemed to him an instrument easier to handle than the three class electoral system, which the bourgeoisie had got control of, and in the first two classes of which it had created for itself an impregnable stronghold.

The history of the Prussian three class electoral system is interesting because it shows so plainly how the most craftily planned political schemes of reactionists can be overthrown by economic development and temporarily turned so as to have an opposite effect from that intended. Designed with cunning shrewdness to bar out all democratic or opposition elements, it answered this purpose perfectly for a decade, until one fine day the bourgeoisie, having grown economically strong and being provoked by the disgusting orgies of landlord and police stewardship began to feel its political strength; it came upon the idea that it only needed to will the thing in order to obtain a majority in the first two electoral classes, and thereby win a victory in the election of the deputies. The idea was made a reality, and Prince Bismarck damned the machinery which so outrageously refused to work as it was expected to; the three class electoral system then became the "most wretched of all electoral systems; " but on the other hand, universal, equal and direct suffrage, this God-be-with-us of the "frantic year" 1848, and which in Napoleonic France had shown such splendid results, now beamed as a brilliant salvation of the state and of society through Caesarism.

So we got the universal franchise; and for another reason as well. The dynastic-feudal revolution from above which topped off Bismarck's "national" policy, would have hung in mid-air unless there had been given to it at least the appearance of a revolution from below. He needed the people even though only for a dummy; and there was no better bait than the universal franchise of 1848. It united the Bismarckian revolution from above with the '48er revolution from below and put the unthinking masses in the delusion that Prussia, enlarged at the expense of Germany and turned into a landlord, police and soldier state, was the realization of German democracy. To-day we know how deep this delusion had taken root; it required decades of brutal misgovernment to root it out again.

But in one thing Bismarck miscalculated, viz.: in the strength of the revolutionary idea. What was possible in France after the battle of June, which drove the whole bourgeoisie into the wildest reactionism, was not possible in Germany where the power of the state was not so closely centralized and where, fed by the development of capitalism, a healthy workingmen's movement grew up which was determined to exploit the national and dynastic crises and struggles in the interest of the proletariat; to make socialism the decisive power in Germany and to help it on to victory and supremacy. The German proletariat had the advantage of being able to draw practical lessons from the labor movement in other countries which were (and are) ahead of Germany in political and economic development. It also had the extraordinary good fortune to be led into the field of political action by its great teachers, Marx, Engels and Lassalle, right at the beginning of its career. It was thereby spared from the errors of pure and simple unionism on the one hand, and of aimless, planless, through and through bourgeois-anarchistic plotting and bawling for revolutions on the other hand. Though the German working-class in 1867, when the universal franchise went into effect, was only to a very small extent filled with class consciousness, it was nevertheless the only class, and the socialist party was the only party, which clearly saw the meaning of voting and the value of the franchise. There was even a slight overestimation of it, but this was useful because it increased the enthusiasm.

If Prince Bismarck entertained the hope that the universal franchise could be exploited in Napoleonic style and that the Reichstag would remain what I called it in 1887, the figleaf to partly cover the naked figure of absolutism, the political basis of this hope was overthrown by the expansion of the North German Confederation into the German Empire. The highest triumph of Bismarckian politics carried its downfall and bankruptcy within it. What the stiff Prussian military and police spirit could perhaps have prevented for an indefinite time within the limits of the North German Confederation, viz.: the rise and growth of an independent popular movement, this could not be prevented on the larger field of the German Empire. The power of the people could not be suppressed, and the jealousy of the "Federal Princes" at Prussian supremacy helped along, so that the trees of Bismarck's feudal Caesarism could not shoot up as high as the trees of Napoleon's prefect-Caesarism. It was not possible by any allurements to take from the workingmen the recognition of the inseparability of socialism from democracy and of democracy from socialism.

"The question" (thus I began my speech in 1869), "what attitude should the Social Democracy take in the political struggle, is answered with ease and certainty if we have attained a clear conception of the inseparability of socialism and democracy. Socialism and democracy are not the same, but they are only different expressions of the same fundamental idea. They belong to each other, round out each other, and can never stand in contradiction to each other. Socialism without democracy is pseudo-socialism, just as democracy without socialism is pseudo-democracy. The democratic state is the only possible form of a socialistically organized society."

This truth, the inseparableness of democracy and socialism, served for the German working class as a sure guide amidst the greatest confusion of political issues, so that the dangerous shoals of state socialism were avoided towards which the Prussian reaction was headed even in the '40s; for the ideal of the garrison and police state was of course a garrison and police socialism, which is euphemistically called state socialism. The sophisms of Wagener and von Schweitzer that democracy has something bourgeois about it, and that socialism, being directed against bourgeois society, must consequently be anti-democratic, did, it, is true, confuse many a man in von Schweitzer's time; but it never found acceptance among the mass of laborers. This pseudo-logic bobbed up again recently in the well known militia debate, but has no longer any significance.

WHAT IS A COMPROMISE?

Before we go farther we must get a clear idea of the meaning of the word "compromise," otherwise every debate on it will be completely without aim and without result, because every one will have in mind something different and consequently no one will meet the arguments of another. If compromise is understood as a concession of theory to practice, then our entire life and activity is a compromise and all human history and the history of the race from the life of the individual up to that of nations and of mankind is an endless, unbroken chain of compromises. That conception of history according to which *tabula rasa*, i.e., a clean sweep, is temporarily made and must be made in order to start a new administration and system free from the old, is in the highest degree unscientific and stands in the most direct contradiction to experience. The clean sweep theory is a spook which exists to-day only in the heads of police politicians who accuse us of wanting to "ruinate" everything that does not fit into our scheme. These gentlemen thereby give judgment against themselves, for they think they are the ones who possess this magical power of being able to "ruinate" anything and everything which Time's eternal loom has woven and is weaving, if perchance it has been done without first getting a permit from the chief of police. The framers of the anti-socialist law and penitentiary law display by their foolish activity only their bottomless ignorance. The organic laws according to which political and social development goes on, cannot be arbitrarily changed or nullified, just as little as this can be done with the laws under which an animal or a plant grows and develops. Whoever interferes there with violence can only disturb and destroy; this has always been the effect wrought by the police politicians. What these fuddlers, who call themselves "statesmen," say against us social democrats, viz.: that we cannot create anything, but only destroy is simply the reflection of their own actings and doings; there is not among the innumerable sins and vices, of which they accuse us, a single one which they have not taken from themselves.

To add one new example to the old ones, I will simply refer to the charge, which has been stereotyped for twenty years, viz.: that the Social Democracy has for its object a proletarian dictatorship. The truth is that since the battle of June at Paris, that is for fifty-one years, we have actually had on the continent of Europe the dictatorship of the bourgeoisie. A dictatorship which has been exercised with fire and sword against the working class; which, after the battle of June, brought us the horrible butcheries of the Commune, and hundreds of smaller butcheries of laborers; a dictatorship which extends to the disfranchisement of the working class and deprives the proletariat of the enjoyment not only of political rights, but also of simple legal rights; a dictatorship which has expressed itself in dozens of exceptional laws and force laws and which we Germans have to thank for the Anti-Socialist law, the penitentiary bill and class law decrees such as the Loebtau judgment and the perjury trial at Essen. And if "King Stumm," who is now king in the realm of "social reform," should accomplish his purpose of annihilating every organization of workingmen, what in comparison with such a dictatorship would be the dictatorship of a Marius or a Sulla or of the French convention of 1792-1794? The political power which the social democracy aims at and which it will win, no matter what its enemies may do, *has not for its object the establishment of a dictatorship of the proletariat, but the suppression of the dictatorship of the bourgeoisie.* Just as the class struggle which the proletariat carries on is only a counter struggle in self defense *to resist the class struggle of the bourgeoisie against the proletariat*; and the end of this struggle by the victory of the proletariat will be the abolition of the class struggle in every form.

We Social Democrats know that the laws according to which political and social evolution goes on can no more be changed or stopped by us than by the authorities of capitalistic society. We know that we can no more introduce at will socialistic production and a socialist form of society than the German Kaiser nine years ago could carry out his February proclamations against the representatives of the capitalistic class struggle. Therefore we were able to watch with smiling indifference the attempt of our opponents to crush the labor movement by force. We were and still are sure of our success, as sure as of the solution of a mathematical problem. But we know also that the shifting of relations, though it goes on unceasingly, yet goes on gradually because it is an *organic movement*; and it goes on, too, without destruction of the existing relations (the removal of the dead is not destruction). The destruction of the existing, of the living, is in general impossible. We saw that plainly in the French revolution, which was probably the best planned and most energetically carried out of all political upheavals; but nevertheless after the "golden period" of ideological groping around and of phantastic and utopian illusions was past, it was compelled to take things as they were and fit the new on to the old. In the first rush it may be possible occasionally to crowd out the living; but history teaches us that the most revolutionary and despotic governments were finally compelled by the logic of facts to yield and to recognize perhaps in another form, that which was unnaturally and mechanically abolished. In short, viewed historically, the present is, as a rule, a compromise between the past and the future.

Therefore to reject a compromise in this sense would be unscientific folly. And practical folly it would be for a political party to fail to draw advantages out of the opportunities of political life and utilize for itself the quarrels of the different opposing parties. Prudence demands this; principles do not come into the question; no obligations are assumed and not to do what prudence demands would be stupidity. That we, Social Democrats in the Reichstag sometimes on a socio-political question vote with the Conservatives for the government, and on political and commercial questions sometimes vote with the Radicals against the government, that is a common requirement of political warfare. Though it is undoubtedly a compromise between theory and practice, it has nothing at all in common with the compromises against which the party has repeatedly declared itself distinctly and expressly. What the party had in mind and what it by formal resolutions made the duty of the members, was the avoidance of alliances, agreements, arrangements, contracts or whatever they might be called, which would involve a surrender of principles or in general a change in the relation of our party towards the bourgeois parties in a manner injurious to us. This last point must be especially emphasized, because the question hinges principally on this. In the debate on taking part in the Prussian legislative elections the question at issue was exclusively this last point; for none of those who advocated participation had the slightest idea of sacrificing party principles in an alliance with the Progressive party, though it must not be overlooked that questions of tactics very easily shift into questions of principle.

If the circumstances and necessities of the situation demand coöperation with other parties, this can always be accomplished without a compromise. I take for example

Belgium. The Liberal party had there a common interest with the Socialist party in fighting the Clericals. The two parties united and worked together up to a certain point. That would have been done even without any fusion. But it was done by fusion, and what was the results? Quarrel and strife. Fusions have shown themselves to be entirely superfluous. When that point is passed up to which community of interests existed and up to which the community of interests, without any fusion, would have induced united action, then united action ceases. If class consciousness is not strong enough among laborers, it certainly is among the gentlemen of the bourgeoisie, in whom the class instinct is much more active than in laborers. And this is true even in countries with democratic laws and institutions. I refer to the separation between bourgeois democrats and socialists in Switzerland, Bernstein's Eldorado, where, according to Bernstein's doctrine, class antagonism should properly have entirely disappeared; but we know it exists there just as strong as in less democratic countries. But it is not denied that the acuteness of class struggles is lessened by democratic institutions.

In Belgium with its free institutions on one hand and its priest-ridden government on the other hand, election alliances between the Social Democracy and the bourgeois parties have heretofore found a fertile soil. At any rate, in all alliances which it formed there our party had the advantage of being in the lead. It could not be exploited nor deceived. And yet the Belgium comrades have found a drawback in compromises. Comrade Vandervelde, writing in the **Wiener Arbeiterzeitung**, welcomes the introduction of the proportional system in Belgium as the end of election alliances. "In future," he writes, "secondary factors will no longer enter into the class struggle; the confusing side issues will disappear which render it so difficult for the masses to grasp the truth of the class struggle." Friend Vandervelde has therefore found out that compromises, even there where they take place under conditions and circumstances the most favorable for the laborers, have an injurious effect because *they render it difficult for the masses to grasp the truth of the class struggle;*" in other words, alliances by removing the laborers from the ground of the class struggle take away from them the possibility of developing their full power and making it count. This they are only able to do on the platform of the class struggle.

The harm of a compromise does not consist in the danger of a formal selling out or side-tracking of party principles. That has probably never been intended by any one in our party. Even when our comrades in Essen in the election before the last voted for the "cannon king" out of spite, they had no idea of surrendering even one iota of our program. The danger and root of the evil does not lie here. It lies in giving up, keeping in the background or forgetting the *class struggle basis, for this is the source of the whole modern labor movement.* It is necessary here to distinguish sharply, and not be misled by catchwords; in short, we must have an emancipation from phrases, as I said decades ago, with reference to the phraseology of anarchism, which poses as revolutionary, but in fact is only small bore reactionism, merely a late-arrival caricature of the bourgeois ideal of freedom and a theatrical masquerade of commercial free competition.

34

Notes

<u>1.</u> **On the Political Stand of the Social Democracy, especially with Reference to the Reichstag**, Berlin 1893, **Vorwaerts** Publishing House.

<u>2.</u> **The Class Struggles in France, 1848-50**, with an Introduction by Frederick Engels, Berlin 1895, **Vorwaerts** Publishing House.

Part 2

SOCIALISM AND ETHICS

Pity for poverty, enthusiasm for equality and freedom, recognition of social injustice and a desire to remove it, is not socialism. Condemnation of wealth and respect for poverty, such as we find in Christianity and other religions, is not socialism. The communism of early times, as it was before the existence of private property, and as it has at all times and among all peoples been the elusive dream of some enthusiasts, is not socialism. The forcible equalization advocated by the followers of Baboeuf, the so-called equalitarians, is not socialism.

In all these appearances there is lacking the real foundation of capitalist society with its class antagonisms. Modern socialism is the *child of capitalist society and its class antagonisms.* Without these it could not be. Socialism and ethics are two separate things. This fact must be kept in mind.

Whoever conceives of socialism in the sense of a sentimental philanthropic striving after human equality, with no idea of the existence of capitalist society, is no socialist in the sense of the class struggle, without which modern socialism is unthinkable. To be sure Bernstein is nominally for the class struggle – in the same manner as the Hessian peasant is for "the Republic and the Grand Duke." Whoever has come to a full consciousness of the nature of capitalist society and the foundation of modern socialism, knows also that a socialist movement that leaves the basis of the class struggle may be anything else, but it is not socialism.

This foundation of the class struggle, which Marx – and this is his immortal service – has given to the modern labor movement, is *the main point of attack in the battle which the bourgeois political economy is waging with socialism*. The political economists deny the class struggle and would make of the labor movement only a part of the bourgeois party movements, and the Social Democracy only a division of the bourgeois democracy. The bourgeois political economy and politics direct all their exertions against the class character of the modern labor movement. If it were possible to create a breach in this bulwark, in this citadel of the Social Democracy, then the Social Democracy is conquered, and the proletariat thrown back under the dominion of capitalistic society. However small such a breach may be in the beginning, the enemy has the power to widen it and the certainty of final victory. And the enemy is most dangerous when he comes as a friend to the fortress, when he slinks in under the cover of friendship, and is recognized as a friend and comrade.

The enemy who comes to us with open visor we face with a

smile; to set our foot upon his neck is mere play for us. The stupidly brutal acts of violence of police politicians, the outrages of anti-socialist laws, the anti-revolution laws, penitentiary bills – these only arouse feelings of pitying contempt; the enemy, however, that reaches out the hand to us for a political alliance; and intrudes himself upon us as a friend and brother, – *him and him alone have we to fear.*

Our fortress can withstand every assault – it can not be stormed nor taken from us by siege – it can only fall *when we ourselves open the doors to the enemy and take him into our ranks as a fellow comrade.* Growing out of the class struggle, our party rests upon the class struggle as a condition of its existence. Through and with that struggle the party is unconquerable; without it the party is lost, for it will have lost the source of its strength. Whoever fails to understand this or thinks that the class struggle is a dead issue, or that class antagonisms are gradually being effaced, stands upon the basis of bourgeois philosophy.

The present discussion over tactics in relation to participation in the elections to the Prussian legislature, has been compared to the discussion which took place among the Social Democratic members of the Reichstag in the middle of the '80s concerning the steamship subsidy. If one examines the matter only superficially the comparison appears strikingly close, but ceases to be so as soon as the kernel of the question is reached. At that time we were concerned with the application of universally recognized principles to a concrete case. That the Social Democratic faction in the Reichstag was interested in the furtherance of German shipping and commercial interests was as universally admitted as that they were opposed to the colonial policy and all other imperialistic reactionary tendencies. The only question was whether the subsidy was primarily in the interest of the German commercial interests, which were national in their character, or whether it was a part of colonial politics that served only the private interests of reactionary individuals at the expense of the public. No one suggested at that time to change the old tactics or alter the course of the party. The present discussion, however, is concerned with the question of a complete change of the old tactics and aims; a change of tactics that would mean a change in the character of the party. It turns upon the question of the retention or abandonment of the class struggle standpoint which distinguishes us from all bourgeois parties; in short, it involves a decisive step, upon which depends whether we shall remain a socialist party, or whether we shall bridge over the Rubicon of the class struggle and become the left wing of the bourgeois democracy.

THEORETICAL DIFFERENCES OF OPINION, NOT MATERIAL: TACTICS IS MATERIAL

Diversity of opinions on theoretical points is never dangerous to the party. There are for us no bounds to criticism, and however great our respect may be for the founders and pioneers of our party, we recognize no infallibility and no other authority than science, whose sphere is ever widening and continually proves what it previously held as truths to be errors; destroys the old decayed foundations and creates new ones; does not stand still for an instant; but in perpetual advance moves remorselessly over every dogmatic belief. At the Union Convention held at Gotha twenty-four years ago I said, "We recognize no infallible Pope, not even a literary one." And when in 1891, in Erfurt, I explained and advocated the newly drafted platform, which was unanimously adopted, I declared that just because our program was a scientific one it must be constantly changed at minor points to meet the continuous advance of science. And I maintain that no man – Marx, in spite of his comprehensive and deep intellect, as little as any other – can bring science to final perfection; and this position is for everyone who understands the nature of science a foregone conclusion. No socialist, therefore, has the right to condemn attacks on the theoretical ideas of the Marxian teachings or to excommunicate any one from the party because of such attacks. But it is wholly different when such attacks imply a complete overturning of our whole conception of society, as, for example, is the case with Bernstein. Then vigorous defense is in order.

Far more dangerous than theoretical assaults are practical disavowals of our principles. Theoretical discussions interest only a comparatively small portion of our membership; whereas practical disavowal of principles and tactical offenses against the party program touch every party comrade and arouse the attention of every party comrade; and when they are not quickly checked and corrected they bring confusion into the whole party. I do not believe I shall be disputed by any one who is familiar with the circumstances and with the party, when I say that the masses within the party care little for Bernstein's writings. They only find sympathy among those who have formerly held similar views, and they arouse a sensation only among our opponents who wish to see fulfilled their old hopes of a split in the party, or to see the whole Social Democracy go over with drums beating, into the bourgeois camp. I will wager that not ten thousand of our comrades have ever read Bernstein's book, and I am far from considering it as a reproach to the party that they show no inclination to busy themselves once more with the underbrush that the founders of socialism, more than a generation ago, yes, in some cases more than two generations ago, hewed down in clearing the way for socialism. One might just as well accuse our comrades of being unscientific because they no longer read the antedeluvian writings of Schultze-Delitzsch that may be lying around somewhere in country villages as dust-covered and shopworn goods.

Look at the list of those who have commented on Bernstein's book. There is not a single laborer among them. It is only those comrades whose professional duty it is to read and discuss such writings. With what interest, on the contrary, the whole party followed the question of participation in the Prussian legislative elections, or the election alliance in Bavaria – how lively was the discussion! This lively interest showed the maturity of the party. We are past the stage of theoretical debates about platforms. The establishment, elaboration and clarifying of our program we leave to science, which in our present society is the business of only a few. But the practical application of our program, and the tactics of the party are the business of all; here all work together.

The supreme importance of tactics and the necessity of maintaining its class struggle character, is something the party has been well conscious of from the beginning. If we read the proceedings of the early conventions held in the '70s we find that in all questions of tactics the thought was continually kept in the foreground that the party must be kept clean from all mixture with all other parties, every one of which, no matter how much they differed from each other or how furiously they fought among themselves, stood upon the ground of bourgeois society as a common basis. This separation of the Social Democracy from all other parties, this essential difference, which silly opponents take as a reason or pretext for declaring us political outlaws, is our pride and our strength.

In the Hamburg convention, where under the influence of a series of confusing circumstances, the mass of the delegates appeared decided to break with the old tactics and traditions, the party still recovered itself at the last moment before the leap into the dark and declared itself by an overwhelming majority as opposed to every compromise. And this resolution has remained in force to the present day. If two or three election districts have been induced to enter into an alliance with a bourgeois party, this was done upon their own responsibility and in undoubted violation of the Hamburg resolution, which, let me repeat, was not repealed by the Stuttgart resolution. On the other hand, the Berlin comrades, who have been complained of by the friends of compromise as violators of the Hamburg resolution, have conscientiously followed the spirit and letter of it, and by their decisive stand maintained the authority of the supreme party council and performed a service to the party.

The advocates of compromise tactics overestimate the value of parliamentary activity and parliamentary representation. Not that I do not recognize the enormous value of parliamentary activity, but this is not an end, but only a means to an end. Our power is not measured by the number of representatives, but by the total number of votes that are behind us.

It is a bourgeois feeling to overvalue the possession of representatives. In representation as in money there is power – power over others. Whoever places the purity and the greatness of our party above all else, for him representatives have value only in so far as they serve to give expression to the power and extent of Social Democracy. What do ten, what do a hundred representatives signify, when our escutcheon has lost its gloss through their acquisition? The value of a representative is small. But the value of the integrity of our party is immeasurable. *In it rests our strength.* As with the shorn hair, that signified his manhood's honor, the strength of Samson disappeared, so the strength of our party would cease if we allowed the bourgeois Delilahs to flatter away our most precious jewel and the roots of our triumphal strength – the party purity, the party honor.

WE ARE A PECULIAR PEOPLE

We may not do as other parties, because we are not like the others. We are – and this cannot be too often repeated – separated from all other parties by an insurmountable barrier, a barrier that any individual can easily surmount; but once on the other side of it, and *he is no Social Democrat.*

We are different from the others; "we are other than the others." What for the others are necessities and conditions of life are death to us. What is it that has made of us in Germany the pivotal party, which according to the significant testimony of Caprivi and the teaching of daily experience makes us the axle around which governmental politics turns? Most assuredly not our representatives in the Reichstag. We might have three times as many representatives, and the allied bourgeois parties would have nothing to fear from us. No, it is the avalanche-like increase of our supporters that gradually, with the certainty of a natural law, or more correctly of a natural force, grows from tens of thousands to hundreds of thousands, and from hundreds of thousands to millions, and is daily increasing, bidding defiance to our opponents and driving them into impotent rage. And this avalanche-like increase has come, and is coming, as a consequence of our opposition to and struggle with all other parties.

All who are weary and heavy laden; all who suffer under injustice; all who suffer from the outrages of the existing bourgeois society; all who have in them the feeling of the worth of humanity, look to us, turn hopefully to us, as the only party that can bring rescue and deliverance. And if we, the opponents of this unjust world of violence, suddenly reach out the hand of brotherhood to it, conclude alliances with its representatives, invite our comrades to go hand in hand with the enemy whose misdeeds have driven the masses into our camp, what confusion must result in their minds! How can the masses longer believe on us? If the men of the clerical party, of the progressive party, and the other boodle parties are our comrades, wherefore then the struggle against capitalist society, whose representatives and champions all of these are? What reason have we, then, for existence? It must be that for the hundreds and thousands, for the millions that have sought salvation under our banner, it was all a colossal mistake for them to come to us. If we are not different from the others, then we are not the right ones – the Savior is yet to come; and the Social Democracy was a false Messiah, no better than the other false ones!

Just in this fact lies our strength, that we are not like the others, and that we are not only not like the others, and that we are not simply different from the others, but that we are their deadly enemy, who have sworn to storm and demolish the Bastile of Capitalism, whose defenders all those others are. Therefore we are only strong when we are alone.

This is not to say that we are to individualise or to isolate ourselves. We have never lacked for company, and we never shall so long as the fight lasts. On the essentially true but literally false phrase about a "single reactionary mass," the Social Democracy has never believed since it passed from the realm of theory to that of practice. We know that the individual members and divisions of the "single reactionary mass" are in conflict with each other, and we have always used these conflicts for our purposes. We have used opponents against opponents, but have never allowed them to use us. We have in the person of Bismarck, the agrarian, fought personified capitalism and militarism and utilized all his capitalistic opponents to weaken him; thus we have used particularism; and thus the bourgeois democracy. That was, however, no compromise, not even a momentary truce. Just as little as it is a compromise or momentary truce when we in the Reichstag vote against the Agrarians in favor of some measure of the Progressive party.

This exclusiveness of the German Social Democracy as opposed to other parties is especially required of us, because of the historical development and political conditions of Germany. We have no revolutionary bourgeois with whom we might temporarily unite as in France and Belgium.

We have no Democratic institutions that make it possible for a Social Democrat to take part in the government side by side with members of other parties. In Switzerland the government is little more than an administration, and one chosen by the people at that. A Social Democrat, as a member of the government of a canton signifies little more than a Social Democrat in a common council. Accordingly our comrades in Switzerland could vote unreservedly for the government monopoly of grain and brandy without feeling that the money secured thereby would be squandered for purposes hostile to the people and injurious to the community.

44

Even in France things are somewhat different from here, although the government is emphatically a class government (occasionally so in a degree scarcely equaled by any other government); yet the relations are so little consolidated, and the influence of the democracy and of the social democracy is so great that any permanent misuse of the governmental powers for reactionary and oppressive purposes is not to be feared. Accordingly it was possible a few years ago for the socialist Jaures to introduce a bill in the legislative chamber regarding the grain traffic, which was externally but little different from the bill introduced in the German Reichstag by Count Kanitz of the Agrarian party. Yet the inner difference was all the greater. In France there is no agrarian class; the bourgeoisie rules directly, yet under conditions that would prevent it from making the means of government – police, army and class judiciary – the end and purpose of the state, as in Germany is not only possible, but is the actual case. We here come again and again upon the tragical fate that robbed Germany of the liberal stage of political development. We have, to be sure, a capitalist class state, and that in the worst sense of the word, but the bourgeois capitalism only rules indirectly; it has to be satisfied to let the purely Catholic clerical party, the Center, hold the balance of power in the German house of representatives, and to let the Prussian agrarian class, a backward anachronistic class, that has no essential function to fulfill either in political or economic life, and has a purely parasitical existence, control the administration. The result of this is that the social democracy of Germany must fulfill the role of champions of political freedom. The task of uniting the struggle for economic independence with that for political liberty has fallen upon the German laboring class; in other words, besides performing its own class mission, it must do what in normally developed lands was long ago done by the bourgeoisie.

THE INCLINED PLANE OF COMPROMISE

All parties without exception recognize us as a political power, and exactly in proportion to our power. Even the craziest reactionary that denies us the right of existence courts our favor and by his acts gives the lie to his words. From the fact that our assistance is sought by other parties, some of our comrades draw the strange conclusion that we should reverse the party tactics, and in place of the old policy of the class struggle against all other parties, substitute the commercial polities of log rolling, wire pulling and compromise. Such persons forget that the power which makes our alliance sought for, even by our bitterest enemies, would have had absolutely no existence were it not for the old class struggle tactics. If Marx, Engels and Lassalle had accepted from Bernstein and his modest or not modest fellow thinkers the tactics of compromise and dependence upon bourgeois parties, then there never would have been any Social Democracy; we would have been simply the tail of the Progressive party. That we accept as a part of our tactics the utilization of the quarrels among the bourgeois parties is self-explaining. And this course has been followed ever since we have had a German Social Democracy. To recognize this, we do not need the counsel of the newly baked party statesmen. That we have here and there worked with the Center or the Progressive party against a reactionary governmental party is understood by the comrades without the necessity of a special party manifesto. And in different election districts we have obtained greater advantages by co-operation with the Center party without fusion than through the recent alliance in Bavaria. One rule does not fit every case.

We Social Democrats dare not be like the other parties, all of whom are equally guilty of the injustices of the present system and equally responsible for them. Every one who suffers under these injustices looks to us for deliverance. Every one of us has had these victims of society after failing to get justice from the courts, from the government, from the Emperor himself, and from all the other parties, come to us as the last and only ones that can help them. They do not know our scientific program; they do not know what capital and capitalism mean; but they have the belief, the feeling, that we are a party that can help when all other parties fail. This belief is for us an inexhaustible source of power. It was a similar faith of despair that spread more and more in the decaying Roman empire and slowly undermined the heathen world until it finally collapsed. We give up this inexhaustible source of power if we ally ourselves with other parties and drive suffering humanity from us by saying to it: "We are not essentially different from the others." Once the boundary line of the class struggle is wiped away and we have started upon the inclined plane of compromise, there is no stopping. Then we can only go down and down until there is nothing deeper. We have had many instructive experiences of this in the Reichstag. Practical polities compelled us to make concessions to the society in which we lived. But every step on the way of concessions to present society was hard for us, and was only done with reluctance. There are some who ridicule us for this. But he who fears to take a step on the inclined plane is at all events a more trustworthy comrade than he who pours out scorn upon the cautious one.

The catch word "revolution" is certainly ridiculous. Ridiculous it certainly is – and no one has expressed this more clearly than I myself – to drop the words "revolution" and "revolutionary" out of the mouth at every opportunity. It can become as mechanical a song as saying one's beads. But ridiculous as it is to boast of belonging to the party and to express one's views at every opportunity when there is no necessity for it, still such exaggerations do not justify us in throwing away the good with the bad, and declaring that to emphasize the revolutionary character of our party is, under all circumstances, ridiculous. To emphasize it is a very serious and a very necessary thing. It is serious, because membership in the social democracy means a struggle, a political struggle with grievous persecutions, and a private struggle for existence, a struggle that for the majority is far more difficult and heavy than the political struggle. And it is *necessary*, because the courage for this twofold struggle is created only by the consciousness that the injustice of society by which the great majority of mankind are to-day oppressed, corrupted and crippled, can only be abolished through a revolutionary movement, that is, a movement that shall completely exterminate capitalism with every fiber of its roots.

I know that it has here and there become the fashion to laugh at the warning about sliding down inclined planes. They refer us to the fable of the sheep and the wolf. The comparison limps, however, and finally turns against the laugher. The wolf was actually there and at last broke into the fold. And in our case it is also no imaginary danger from which we are warned. And at all events the interests of the party are at least as carefully guarded by the warners as by the scorners. Heretofore distrust was counted as a democratic virtue, and over-confidence as a democratic vice. Here and there are found persons who would reverse this maxim.

48

BLUECHER'S MOTTO

The proletariat stands politically as well as socially in the most abrupt contradiction to the present class state. It must fight it on all fields and upon every question, both of domestic and of foreign policy. To be sure it is not always easy to decide rightly. Where the interests are not clearly visible the feelings may be easily deceived. Fortunately we have at the points where it is hardest to decide an infallible compass in the actions of our enemies. If there are questions on which we can temporarily unite with them it is still inconceivable that anything that is fought for by our enemies as a question of great importance, or especially as of vital importance to them, can be desirable for the proletariat. We shall never go wrong if we do what is opposed to the interests of our enemy. On the other hand, we shall almost never go right if we do what our enemies applaud. Historical development is a continuous conflict, a conflict of interests, a conflict of races, a conflict of classes. And if friendship does not count even in ordinary business, how much less so in such a conflict. Good-naturedness and sentimentality have no place in politics. They have never won a victory, but have brought unnumbered defeats. Bluecher's motto, "Always follow the cannon's roar and throw yourself upon the enemy," is the best rule also in political warfare.

Just a word in this connection. The class instinct of the bourgeoisie is far better developed than that of the proletariat. The governing class naturally knows its interests better than the governed, who have so much less opportunity to become informed and are also sometimes intentionally, and sometimes not, systematically deceived and misled from a recognition of their interests. Do not say that it is the rough form in which socialism is often set forth that frightens and embitters the bourgeoisie. That is absolutely false. It is not the form; it is the content which they detest; and the more harmless the form so much the more dangerous do the contents appear to the gentlemen of the bourgeoisie. The fineness of the form makes no difference to them. That is clear from the manner in which they fight out their quarrels among themselves.

What a lot of abuse and fiction has been brought out about "Toelke's club!" "Toelke's club" really never touched any one ungently. But club tactics has existed in Germany for decades, and has even yet not wholly disappeared. But it is not laborers and also not socialists with whom the club counts, as the *ultimo ratio*, the conclusive argument. It is the tactics of the noblest of the nation, the national liberals, who in the middle and southwestern portions of Germany organized battalions of brawling club heroes, and thereby sought to retain their political domains through a brutal terrorism. But the advancing social democracy has well nigh stamped them out.

COMPROMISES LIKE TREATIES ARE NOT KEPT

At any rate we may be sure that the political instinct of our bourgeois opponents, as soon as their class interests come into play, will lead them to take a position hostile to us. A classical example is furnished by Belgium, where, as already remarked, a compromise was concluded under the most favorable circumstances conceivable, between the socialists and the liberals. Our party was in undisputed possession of the leadership and was therefore in no danger of being cheated out of the fruits of the common victory. The end sought was universal, equal and direct suffrage. But the clerical party knows its boys, knows its Pappenheimers. It knows that the bourgeoisie has no class interest in giving the laborers, who, in modern industrial states, constitute a majority of the population, the universal suffrage and thereby the prospect of winning a majority and getting political supremacy. It made a counter demand for proportional representation with plural voting, that is, giving more votes to the rich, and thereby granting to the radical bourgeoisie a share in the government, if it would assist in defeating universal and direct suffrage. And behold, without a minute's hesitation the gentlemen of the radical bourgeoisie broke their agreement with the socialists and joined the clericals in their fight against universal suffrage and the social democracy. Whoever is not convinced by this example that the emancipation struggle of the proletariat is a class struggle is one on whom further arguments would be wasted.

There is no political party upon whose firm support the social democracy can reckon. And every assistance that we can possibly expect from bourgeois parties in the complications of political life must, if we act skillfully, come to us anyhow without compromise. It is the same with compromises and fusions between parties as with treaties between nations. They are observed so long, and only so long, as they are in the interest of the parties concerned. When common interests exist, however, no compromise, fusion or contract is necessary. Suppose, to cite an actual instance, suppose the securing of six more representatives in the legislature was of great importance to our party in Bavaria; with the strength and influence which our party had it could have found a way to get them without any "cattle trade." The strengthening of the Center party, aside from the question of principles, was a great tactical error. This error was all the greater in that it checked the process of dissolution which the Center party is now undergoing. This party holds together so long as the laborers who come within the sphere of its influence have not yet attained to class consciousness, have not yet learned to set their class interests above their sectarian interests; this is a process which the economic development necessarily carries along with itself, and which we aim to hasten by our propaganda. In Offenbach and other election districts this has been so far attained that in the last election the majority of the Catholics voted for our candidates on the first ballot instead of for the candidates of their own party. The class struggle tactics is not only more correct in principle; it is also more practical and successful than compromise tactics.

The standpoint of utility, which was emphasized by the advocates of the Bavarian compromise, is certainly a very useful point, but there are other factors than utility which must be taken into consideration. The purity of our principles, the idealism of our struggle, these are factors of strengthening and drawing power that have given to us courage for all our battles, and have given to our doctrines an irresistible attraction for all who feel themselves oppressed and have a sense of honor. Certainly the alliance with the Center party was very useful; it has given us half a dozen legislative votes; but what is it Gretchen says?

> "How scornfully I once reviled
> When some poor maiden was beguiled!
> More speech than any tongue suffices
> I craved to censure others' vices.
> Black as it seemed I blackened still,
> And blacker yet was in my will;
> And blessed myself and boasted high –
> And now – a living sin am I!"

Yes, how bravely we could once scold at the political log rollers, especially at the black ones! We painted them blacker than black. And to-day? We dare not do all that our opponents do. We dare not sacrifice everything for advantages. For what is an advantage to our opponents is deadly poison to us. The nobility say of themselves, *noblesse oblige*; so we may say, *socialisme oblige*, socialism imposes its obligations.

If tactics prescribes or allows us to obligate ourselves to our opponents in order to attain a temporary success by a temporary alliance, then Schuhmacher in Solingen acted as a good tactician in the opportunist sense by fusing with the Progressive party last year at the Reichstag elections to rescue the party from us. He did not become a bourgeois, not at all; he only used the bourgeoisie to overthrow us, the false socialists, and to help true socialism on to victory, just as Millerand is going to crush out militarism by a compact with Gallifet and Waldeck-Rousseau. Schuhmacher can give exactly the same reasons for his action as Millerand can for his. Treason to the party is what we call it.

With the growth of Social Democracy and with its entrance into fields hitherto dominated by other parties, and with the extension of our practical activity, we come more and more frequently into momentary unions, or momentary relations with other parties. But these momentary relations must never become momentary alliances. We must never bind the *party*. We must always keep our hand free; exploit the conditions; let our opponents do the dirty work for us; and with the goal of the party firmly in mind, keep in the middle of the road, and go our own way, only going along with opposing parties when our way happens to be the same as theirs. That we are a party of the class struggle, who have nothing in common with any other party, and who have to fight and conquer all other parties, in order to attain our goal, is something which we must never for a moment lose sight of.

MILLERAND

Concerning the case of Millerand, and the question of party union, I wrote at the invitation of the French comrades, on the occasion of the last annual convention of the Labor Party (the Marxists) at Epernay, the following letter:

"Dear Friends: You know that I have made it a rule not to interfere with the affairs of the socialists in other countries. But as you wish to know my opinion on the burning question that is occupying the attention of the whole laboring and socialist portion of France, and as many of your countrymen, who have wholly different views upon this question from yours, have also turned to me, I have no longer any reason to withhold my opinion. The situation with which you are now occupied in France is at bottom not a foreign affair as to Germans.

"The internationality of socialism is a fact that is daily becoming more evident and more significant. We socialists are one nation to ourselves, – one and the same international nation in all the lands of the earth. And the capitalists with their agents, instruments and dupes are likewise an international nation, so that we can truthfully say, there are to-day only two great nations in all lands that battle with each other in the great class struggle, which is the new revolution – a class struggle on one side of which stands the proletariat, representing socialism, and on the other the bourgeoisie, representing capitalism.

"While the bourgeois world of capitalism continues and the bourgeoisie rules, so long are all states necessarily class states, and all governments class governments, serving the purposes and interests of the ruling class, and destined to lead the class struggle for the bourgeoisie against the proletariat – for capitalism against socialism, for our enemies and against us. From the standpoint of the class struggle which is the foundation of militant socialism, that is a truth which has been raised by the logic of thought and of facts beyond the possibility of a doubt. A socialist who goes into a bourgeois government, either goes over to the enemy or else puts himself in the power of the enemy. In any case the socialist who becomes a member of a bourgeois government separates himself from us, the militant socialists. He may claim to be a socialist but he is no longer such. He may be convinced of his own sincerity, but in that case he has not comprehended the nature of the class struggle – does not understand that the class struggle is the basis of socialism.

"In these days, under the rule of capitalism, a government, even if it is full of philanthropy and animated by the best of intentions, can do nothing of real value to our cause. One must keep free from illusions. Decades ago, I said: 'If the way to hell is paved with good intentions, the way to defeat is paved with illusions.' In the present society, a non-capitalist government is an impossibility. The unfortunate socialist who casts in his lot with such a government if he will not betray his class only condemns himself to impotency. The English bourgeoisie offers the best example of weakening the opposition by permitting them to participate in the government. It has become the traditional policy of all parties in England that the most radical member of the opposition who is naive enough to be taken in should be given a place in the government. This man serves as a shield to the government and disarms his friends who cannot shoot at him – just as in battle one may not shoot at the hostages that the enemy has placed in front of itself.

"That is my answer concerning the question of the entrance of a socialist into a bourgeois government.

"Now, as to the second question: The question of unity and agreement. The answer is dictated to me by the interests and principles of the party. I am for the unity of the party – for the national and international unity of the party. But it must be a unity of *socialism and socialists.* The unity with *opponents* – with people who have other aims and other interests, is no *socialist unity.* We must strive for unity at any price and with all sacrifices. But while we are uniting and organizing, we must rid ourselves of all foreign and antagonistic elements. What would one say of a general who in the enemy's country sought to fill the ranks of his army with recruits from the ranks of the enemy? Would that not be the height of foolishness? Very well, to take into our army – which is an army for the class struggle and the class war – opponents, soldiers with aims and interests entirely opposite to our own, – that would be madness, that would be suicide.

"On the ground of the class struggle we are invincible; if we leave it we are lost, because we are no longer socialists. The strength and power of socialism rests in the fact that we are leading a class struggle; that the laboring class is exploited and oppressed by the capitalist class, and that within capitalist society effectual reforms, which will put an end to class government and class exploitation, are impossible.

"We cannot traffic in our principles, we can make no compromise, no agreement with the ruling system. We must break with the ruling system and fight it to a finish. It must fall that socialism may arise, and we certainly cannot expect from the ruling class that it will give to itself and its domination the death blow. The International Workingmen's Association accordingly preached that `The emancipation of the laboring class must be the work of the laborers themselves.'

"Undoubtedly there are bourgeois who from a feeling of justice and humanity place themselves upon the side of the laborers and socialists, but these are only the exceptions; the mass of the bourgeoisie has class consciousness, a consciousness of being the ruling and exploiting class. Indeed, the mass of the bourgeoisie, just because they are a ruling class, have a much sharper and stronger class consciousness than the proletariat.

"I conclude: You have asked my opinion, and I have given it to you. It is for you to do what the interests and principles of the party demand that you should do.

"Fraternal greeting to the convention at Epernay. Long live the France of the socialists and the laborers! Long live international socialism!

"Weimar, Aug. 10, 1899 W. LIEBKNECHT."

I have nothing to add to my letter. The events since then have justified it. The presence of a socialist in the government has accomplished nothing and prevented nothing that could not have been accomplished or prevented without this presence. On the other hand, in so far as the Social Democracy has caused or endorsed the entrance of a socialist into the government it has become in part responsible for all the sins of omission and of commission done by the government during the time in which a socialist was a member.

THE SITUATION IN FRANCE

It may be said in excuse or justification that they have acted under extraordinary conditions, – to rescue the republic, which would otherwise have been lost. This excuse will not stand examination. The republic of France is not upheld by a few men in the government, including the socialist, but by the *French laborers* with whom the greater part of the peasants and small bourgeoisie stand side by side, and also by the great majority of the French people, who do not allow themselves to be led astray by the priests, nor coerced by the reactionary capitalists. Militarism is by far less strong and dangerous in France than in Germany, and the French army is to a much greater extent than in Germany a people's army. The army is as large as in Germany, although the population is fifteen million less; it contains therefore a larger per cent of the total population. France is actually at the point where it must break with the Prussian-German military system which it adopted after the war of 1870-71; it must either do as the minister of war, General Gallifet, has recommended – replace it with a well-drilled Praetorian Guard – or enter at once upon the militia system, and arm every person capable of bearing arms. A *coup d'etat* is impossible with such an army. No matter how reactionary a portion of the officers may be, the mass of soldiers are too close to the people to be used for such purposes.

If, as has been represented to us, the actual formation of the Waldeck-Rousseau Ministry was necessary to protect the republic against a *coup d'etat*, then the republican sentiment of the French proletariat was security enough for the government

– in every way a far better security than the participation of a socialist in the cabinet.

The circumstance that the chief of this ministry was a particularly clear-cut capitalist, and that the Minister of War was one of the most notorious "saberers" of the "Little Napoleon," and one of the most bloodthirsty murderers of the Communists, made the impropriety of Millerand's action all the more evident. But even if in place of Waldeck-Rousseau there had been a genuine Democrat, as for example, Brisson, and in place of Gallifet an honorable soldier not yet stained with laborers' blood, the step would have been no less objectionable from our standpoint, though it would not have wounded the feelings so much.

Class antagonism accompanied by the class struggle is now an existing fact. The state is, so long as this class opposition and class struggle exists, necessarily a class state, and the government of this state, with like necessity, is a class government. The socialist who allows himself to become a member of such a government will soon lose his class-consciousness, if he has not already laid it down at the door of the cabinet, like a Mohammedan does his shoes at the entrance of the mosque, unless he has the courage to seize the first opportunity offered for a conflict and a break.

I do not care to busy myself with the purely scholastic question as to whether a case might ever possibly arise in which a socialist should enter into a non-socialist government. Such an occasion could only arise after a catastrophic overthrow of the state, for example, during the course of a world war, when the government of a class state had broken down without the necessary elements being yet present for the formation of a socialist state.

Such an occasion has certainly not yet arisen in France, and perhaps the last persons whose mission it is to "rescue the Republic" are just these same Waldeck-Rousseau and Gallifet. It is the *Socialist Party* which was and is and remains the only party whose mission it is to be the rescuer and safeguard of the Republic, and this with or without Millerand.

Guesde and Lafargue, the leading representatives of scientific socialism in France, have set forth in a scathing critique of "Ministerial" opportunist socialism, the distinction between the activity of a member of a popularly elected body and an officer of an executive body of the government itself of the established state. The officials and the government are the organs of class rule, who must from their very nature act in the interests of the ruling class. The participation in a popularly elected body (Reichstag, legislature, common council, etc.) is on the contrary an expression of popular sovereignty, which, though it is subject to the influences of the class rule, is really above it, and is the only power that can make an end of it. The representatives of the Social Democracy in such popular bodies are like the basalt blocks, which, pushed up from the interior of the earth, have broken through the sandstone and slate strata: – they arise from the heart of the people, are a part of the people, and have in themselves the right and the power of popular sovereignty, which overtops and dominates all political and social matters. They are not there by the grace of the powers that be, but against their will, and in spite of their power – servants to be sure, but honorable servants, servants, not of the possessors of power, but of the people, who have chosen them to secure the realization of their sovereign will. Therefore, it is fundamentally incorrect to designate our activity in the Reichstag and other representative bodies as a compromise with the ruling powers. To be sure, we have to work there together with our enemies, but as an independent power, exercising the mandates we have received from the people. That is no co-operation upon the basis of common views and aims; it is a labor that is a battle – a mutual struggle, a measuring of forces, whose play, direction and intensity, according to the eternal law of the parallelogram of forces, results in legislation and government.

It is in the nature of things that out of this mutual wrestling and struggle, changing groups and momentary contacts should result; to call such momentary groupings compromises is a pure distortion of terms. A coming together as a result of conditions, and a working and striving in the same direction owing to circumstances, is just as little a contract, an alliance or a compromise, as the reciprocal touching of the pieces of glass in a kaleidoscope is a contract, an alliance or a compromise. Whether the shaking power is a mechanical one, or is the force of organized law is all the same. Such approaches are without any obligations, are productions of the moment, born of the moment and swept away with the moment.

It is no loss incorrect to compare co-operation at second ballotings to such alliances as were proposed for the Prussian legislative elections and as were actually made for the Bavarian elections. Such co-operation is only an episode of the battle at the polls which is fought by the party as a whole. After the first and chief election day an after battle follows, in which the undecided points are fought out. That we, in these subsequent elections in electoral districts where we cannot ourselves put up a candidate, should vote for that one of the opposition candidates whose election offers the most advantages to our party, is a requirement of elementary intelligence. I previously advocated this as an act of self-evident desirability at a time when some of those who are to-day enthusiastic for a participation in the Prussian legislative elections accused me of a half-betrayal of our principles. If, at a time when an exception law exists, or is in sight, we did not give our votes in these special elections to that one of two bourgeois candidates who was opposed to the exception law, we should be asses deserving the cudgel. But that is no compromise. We pledge ourselves to nothing, we sacrifice no principle, we sacrifice no interest; on the contrary, we act solely in our own interest, which we should have injured had we acted otherwise. The obligations rest upon our opponents. This tactics is so simple and natural that it was only brought into question for a time by an unclear hobby-riding of principles; as soon as the party leaders ceased to recommend this tactics, the rank and file of the party, following a sound instinct, carried it out anyhow over the heads of those leaders. And from time to time a special line of action was decided upon for each particular case. No trafficking, no underhand work; open and above board we attack the enemy; and where two enemies stand in opposition, one of whom must win the mandate, we strike the most dangerous of the two to earth. This is a policy of fighting such as befits a fighting party.

In the original elections for the Reichstag, we are a fighting party that by its own strength wins its share in the popular representation. We offer battle front to all parties, not even excepting those for whose members we may vote at the supplemental elections as the interest of our party may require. But in the Prussian legislative elections it is impossible for us to win a single representative by our own strength; in order to gain one or more it is necessary to turn to a bourgeois party and make a political trade with them. In the Reichstag elections we are the strongest party in Germany, but in the Prussian legislative elections we are the weakest of all, indeed, completely helpless; because under the "worst of all election laws" we have, to be sure, a vote, but our vote is rendered nugatory, and a mandate can only be secured under the condition that we become dumb voting cattle of a bourgeois party.

In the Bavarian legislative election things are somewhat different. In Bavaria, the election laws do not make it impossible to secure a mandate. This does not argue in favor of a compromise, but, on the contrary, places the "cattle trade," which took place this summer, in a still worse light.

I will not here enter upon the grounds of opposition to participating in the Prussian legislative election. The demoralization through the change of front in the Reichstag elections and the legislative elections, the confusion in the minds, the loosening of discipline, and above all the obliteration of the class struggle character of our party has been already, and by myself among others, so often and so emphatically set forth that I will not tire the reader by a repetition.

Only one thing more.

If the bourgeois parties still had any vitality left they would not need our help to secure a victory in the Prussian legislative elections. The first two classes belong to the bourgeois electors. No one can rob them of a majority if they do not themselves surrender it. How then can we help them? Can one make the lame or the drunk walk? One can help them up, but as soon as one lets go they fall to the ground like an empty sack. We cannot escape this dilemma; either the bourgeoisie still has political vitality – in which case they do not need our help; or they do not have it, and in that case our help would be useless.

Can we be expected to make an alliance with a corpse?

INDEPENDENT ACTION IS THE ONLY THING THAT IS PRACTICAL

Fault has been found because I said in a newspaper article that a new anti-socialist law would be less evil than the abolition of class antagonism and party lines through fusion with the Prussian Progressive party in the legislative elections. The more I consider it the more I am convinced of the correctness of this position. What is to become of our party if we allow ourselves to be pressed out of the path of our principles by threatened or threatening dangers and disadvantages? Fear is proverbially a poor adviser for human action; for a party it is destruction. Fear of the labor movement and socialism has caused the political downfall of the German bourgeoisie; and the days of the Social Democracy are numbered as soon as the cry of fear finds a response in us. We should not challenge, but we should not sound the alarm and be misled by fear into taking steps that do not accord with the principles, the nature and the honor of our party. One does not disarm an enemy through timidity and gentleness; one simply emboldens him. Not that we should seek to run our heads through a wall. We wish to be and must be "practical." But has this ever been denied or questioned? We have always been "practical," Bernstein to the contrary notwithstanding. We have always based our efforts on existing conditions and worked methodically with our eye upon the goal. In cities, states and empire, all reasonable improvements have at least been supported, if not proposed by the Social Democracy. Think only of the greatest of all reforms, the reform of the social evil, in which the government, if it does not wish to build ruins or air castles, must take hold of the demands made by us over ten years ago.

We can say of ourselves, that not only are we practical, but that we are the only practical party – practical in the sense of reasonable. Only those who recognize the organic laws of development and systematically strive in harmony with them towards a definite goal are practical. And this is the way we work. Our opponents either do not know these laws, or else if they recognize them they seek to bend or break them. Whoever seeks to compel water to run up hill is certainly not practical, and such is the foolish aim of our opponents. To be sure it has been said that the laborers cannot alone secure the emancipation of the laboring class; that the intelligent and cultured elements of the other classes must co-operate with them. We are pointed to the many measures useful to the laboring class which are enacted or supported by the bourgeois parties. But this is sophistical reasoning. For (and on this point the evidence of Bismarck is decisive) none of these social reform measures, and surely they are few enough, would ever have been enacted *without the initiative and the pressure of the proletariat and the Social Democracy.*

Bernstein claims that socialism is the ultimate outcome of liberalism. To claim this is to absolutely deny the existence of any class antagonism.

This sentence was reversed by Miquel, my former comrade *in communismo*, and present Chancellor *in re*, so as to read, Liberalism in the ultimate outcome of communism. And that the liberalism of Miquel is very near to conservatism, in the German sense, that is, to the agrarian medieval ideal of personal bondage, every one knows who has ears to hear and eyes to see.

No, Social Democracy must remain for itself, must seek for and generate its power within itself. Every power outside of ourselves on which we seek to lean is for us only weakness. In the consciousness of our strength, in our faith in the world-conquering mission of socialism lies the secret of our extraordinary, almost miraculous success.

Islam was unconquerable so long as it trusted in itself alone and saw an enemy in every non-Mohammedan. From the moment when Islam entered upon the path of compromise and united with the non-Mohammedan, the so-called civilized powers, its conquering power was gone. With Islam it could not have been otherwise. It was not the true world redeeming faith. Socialism, however, is this, and socialism cannot conquer nor redeem the world if it ceases to believe upon itself *alone*.

Therefore, we will not turn from the old tactics, nor from the old program. Ever advancing with science and economic development, we are what we were and we will remain what we are.

Or – the Social Democracy will cease to exist.

Further reading – Socialist Classics

Unit 1 – Short introductory works

1. The Communist Manifesto (1848) Karl Marx and Friedrich Engels

2. Wage-labour and capital (1847) Karl Marx

3. Value, Price and Profit (1865) Karl Marx

4. Socialism: Utopian and Scientific (1880) Friedrich Engels

5. The German Ideology (1846) Karl Marx and Friedrich Engels

6. Anarchism and Socialism (1895) Georgi Plekhanov

7. No Compromise, No Political Trading (1899) Wilhelm Liebknecht

8. Reform or Revolution (1900) Rosa Luxemburg

9. Leninism or Marxism? (1904) Rosa Luxemburg

10. Socialism Made Easy (1909) James Connolly